Photo

This Book Belongs To

What wonderful news!

On .... Mummy and Daddy found out I was on my way!

Mummy said ....

....

Daddy said ....

....

And then they told Mummy's parents and Daddy's parents.

Everyone was so happy.

Here are pictures of them all smiling and waiting for me.

Photo

Photo

Photo

Photo

Family tree

Grandma

Grandpa

Mummy

Baby

Sisters

Brothers

Grandma
Grandpa
Daddy
Uncles
Aunts
Cousin

All about my family

A letter from Mummy to me

A letter from Daddy to me

First visit to the Doctor

Due date ....

First heart-beat ....

First movement ....

First ultrasound scan ....

Mummy's new routine

Daddy's new routine

Things they did together for me

Shopping

Decorating

Reading books

Child-care classes

My room and things

Photo

Photo

Photo

Photo

The baby shower

Guests and Gifts

Photo

Photo

Photo

Names for me

These are some of the names that Mummy, Daddy and some others thought for me

If I were a girl

If I were a boy

I am here!

Time ....

Place ....

Weight..

Length ....

Eyes ....

Hair ....

People present ....

Mummy's story of my birth

Daddy's story of my birth

My first picture and hospital tag

Photo

Tag

My birth certificate

Birth Certificate

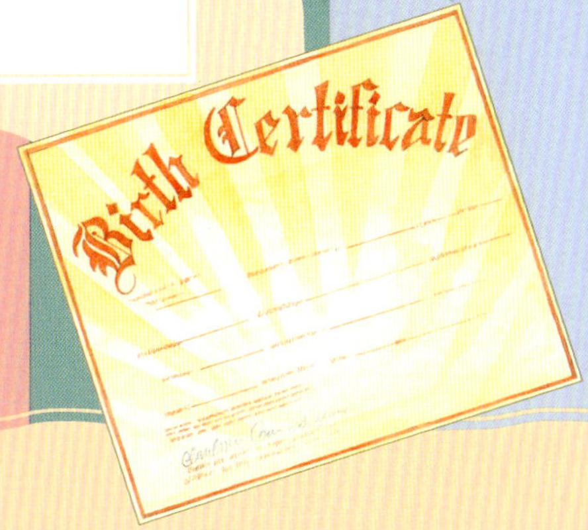

My birth announcement

Birth Announcement

Gifts and Wishes

The day I was named

It's official! My Name is ....

My Nickname is ....

My Godparents are ....

Here are some pictures of my special day.

Photo

Photo

Photo

Photo

My tiny footprints

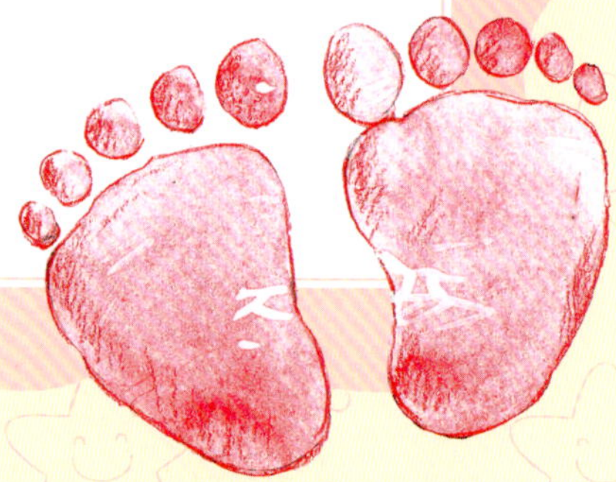

...and tiny hands

Home sweet home!

Mummy, Daddy and I live in ....

....

Other members in the house ....

....

Bathtime

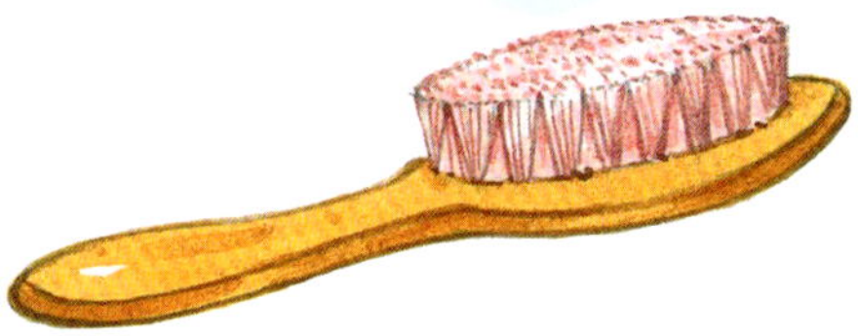

My first bath was on ....

....

and this is what i did ....

....

My favourite bath toys ....

....

Bathtime games I played ....

....

Bedtime

My sleeping times were ....

My favourite lullabies ....

....

My bedtime toys ....

....

Growing Up

My first smile ....

My first laugh ....

I first said mama on ....

I first said dada on ....

I first sat up alone on ....

I first crawled on ....

I first stood up myself on ....

I first walked myself on ....

Mealtime

Foods I love ....

....

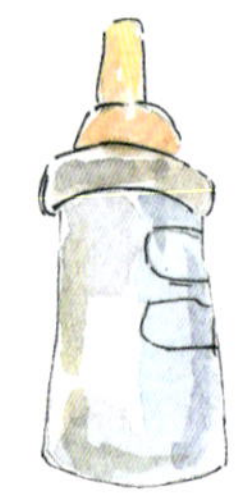

Foods I hate ....

....

Fun and games at mealtime ....

....

Growth Chart

	Birth	Height	Weight
Month-1			
Month-2			
Month-3			
Month-4			
Month-5			
Month-6			
Month-7			
Month-8			
Month-9			
Month-10			
Month-11			
Month-12			

My first tooth

Photo

My first haircut

Photo and a Lock of hair

Outings and vacations

The place we went to ....

We travelled by ....

My favourite outings were ....

My first travel ticket

Travel Ticket

Here are some photographs of my exciting holidays!

Festivities

Some photographs of my first festivals.

Photo

Photo

Photo

Photo

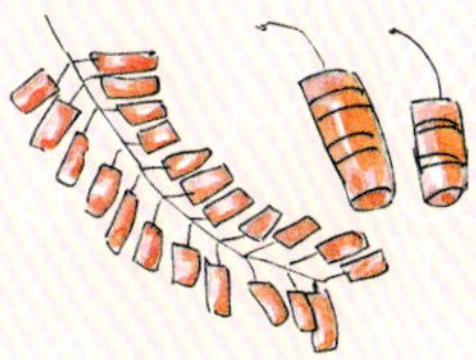

Photo

Photo

Photo

My first birthday

Photographs of my first birthday. It was so much fun!

Photo

Photo

Photo

Photo
Photo

My favourite things

Toys ....

....

Books ....

....

Clothes ....

....

People ....

....

Places ....

....

Little friends ....

....

Games ....

....

Songs ....

....

Rhymes ....

....

Stories ....

....

When I grow up

Mummy wants me to be

Daddy Wants me to be

Moments to Treasure